easy **GUITAR TAB EDITION**

CLASSIC ROCK HITS
FOR EASY GUITAR

T0059230

Alfred

ISBN-10: 0-7390-4202-5
ISBN-13: 978-0-7390-4202-1

CONTENTS

FRIEND OF THE DEVIL

Words by
ROBERT HUNTER
Music by
JERRY GARCIA and JOHN DAWSON

4

Bridge:

Got two rea - sons why I cry___ a - way___ each lone - ly night..

___ The first one's named Sweet Anne Mar - ie, and she's___

[C]

___ my heart's de - light.___ Sec - ond one___ is

[D]

pris - on, ba - by, the sher - iff's on___ my___ trail, and

[Am]

if he catch - es up with me___ I'll spend my life in

[C]

jail.

[D]

Verse 4:

Got a wife in Chi - no, babe,___ and one___ in Cher - o - kee.___

[G]   [C]

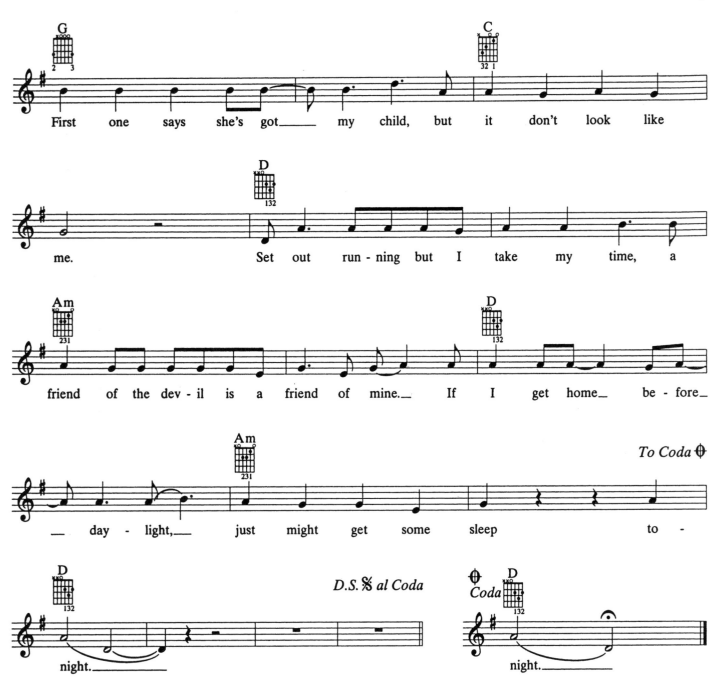

Verse 3:
I ran down to the levee,
But the devil caught me there.
He took my twenty dollar bill
And vanished in the air.
(To Bridge:)

CHINA GROVE

Words and Music by
TOM JOHNSTON

FOR WHAT IT'S WORTH

Words and Music by
STEPHEN STILLS

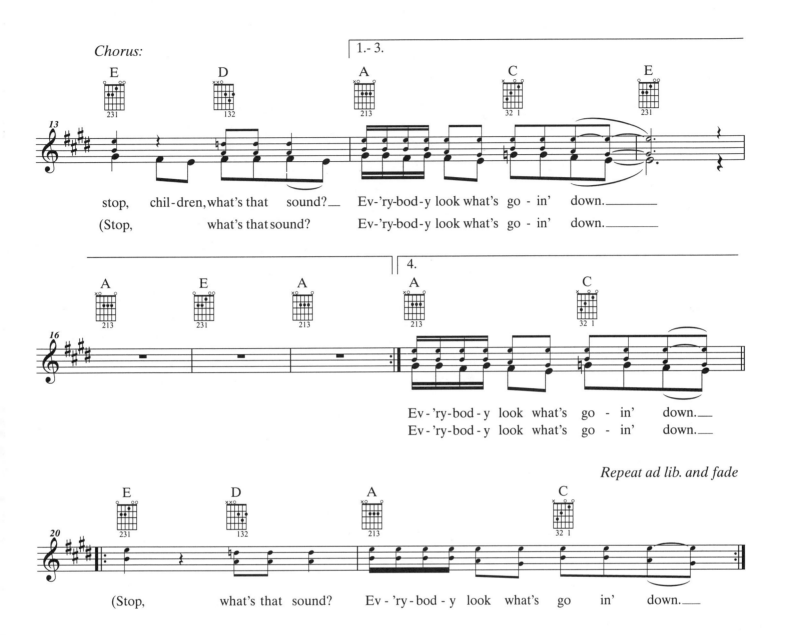

Chorus:

stop,   chil-dren, what's that   sound?__ Ev-'ry-bod-y look what's go - in'   down._____

(Stop,   what's that sound?   Ev-'ry-bod-y look what's go - in'   down._____

Ev-'ry-bod-y look what's go - in'   down.__

Ev-'ry-bod-y look what's go - in'   down.__

Repeat ad lib. and fade

(Stop,   what's that sound?   Ev-'ry-bod-y look what's go   in'   down.__

Verse 2:
There's battle lines being drawn,
Nobody's right if everybody's wrong.
Young people speaking their minds,
Getting so much resistance from behind.
I think it's time we stop...
(To Chorus:)

Verse 3:
What a field day for the heat,
A thousand people in the street.
Singing songs and carrying signs,
Mostly say "Hooray for our side."
It's time we stop...
(To Chorus:)

Verse 4:
Paranoia strikes deep,
Into your life it will creep.
It starts when you're always afraid,
Step out of line, the man come and take you away.
We better stop...
(To Chorus:)

GIMME SOME LOVIN'

Words and Music by
STEVE WINWOOD, MUFF WINWOOD
and SPENCER DAVIS

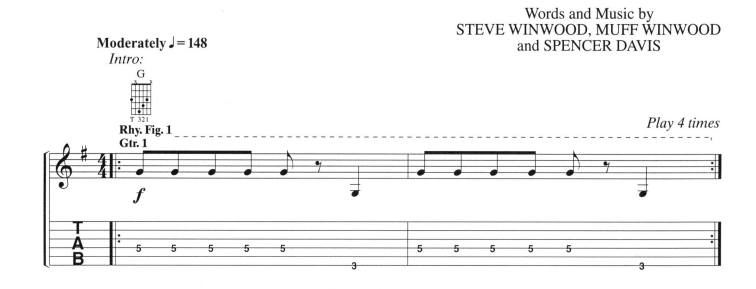

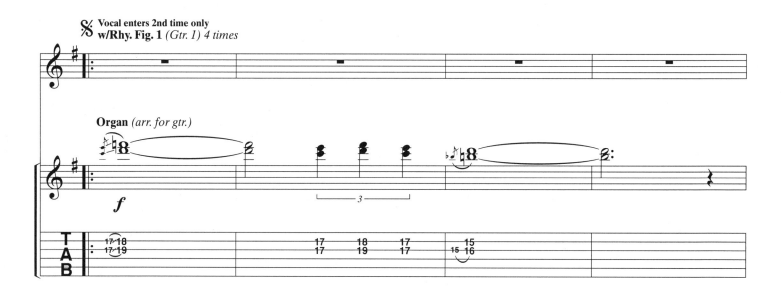

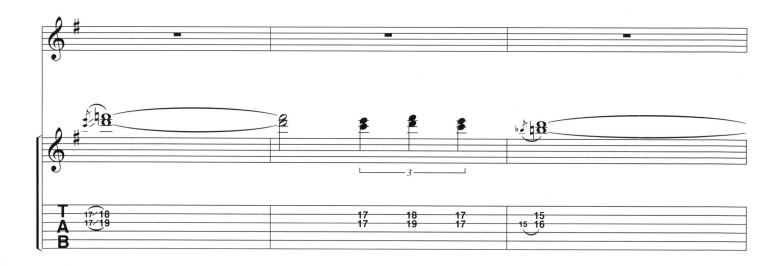

12

I GOT A NAME

Moderately in 2 ♩ = 80
Intro:

Words by NORMAN GIMBEL
Music by CHARLES FOX

*Acous. Gtr. w/capo II, fret numbers relative to capo.

Verse:

1. Like the pine trees lin - in' the wind - ing road, I've got a name,
2. Like the north wind whis - tl - in' down the sky, I've got a song,
3. *See additional lyrics*

___ I've got a name. ___
___ I've got a song. ___

Like the sing - in' bird ___ and the croak - in' toad, I've got a name, ___
Like the whip - poor - will ___ and the ba - by's cry, I've got a song, ___

___ I've got a name. ___
___ I've got a song. ___

I Got a Name - 3 - 1

Instrumental:

And I'm gon-na go___ there free._____

Coda

Mov-in' me down the high-way,

roll-in' me down the high-way, mov-in' a-head so life___ won't___

pass_ me by.___

Verse 3:
Like the fool I am and I'll always be,
I've got a dream, I've got a dream.
They can change their minds but they can't change me,
I've got a dream, I've got a dream.
I know I could share it if you want me to,
If you're going my way, I'll go with you.
(To Chorus:)

HELPLESS

Slow ♩ = 56

Words and Music by
NEIL YOUNG

There is a town in North On - tar - i - o

with dream com - fort, mem - o - ry to spare.

And in my mind I still need a place to go,

all my chang - es were there.

1.2. Blue, blue win - dows be - hind the stars,

yel - low moon on the rise.

A HORSE WITH NO NAME

Words and Music by
DEWEY BUNNELL

Verse 2:
After two days in the desert sun
My skin began to turn red.
After three days in the desert fun
I was looking at a river bed.
And the story it told of a river that flowed
Made me sad to think it was dead.
You see I've...
(To Chorus:)

Verse 3:
After nine days I let the horse run free
'Cause the desert had turned to sea.
There were plants and birds and rocks and things,
There were sand and hills and rings.
The ocean is a desert with it's life underground
And the perfect disguise above
Under the cities lies a heart made of ground
But the humans will give no love.
You see I've...
(To Chorus:)

THE HOUSE OF THE RISING SUN

Words and Music by
ALAN PRICE

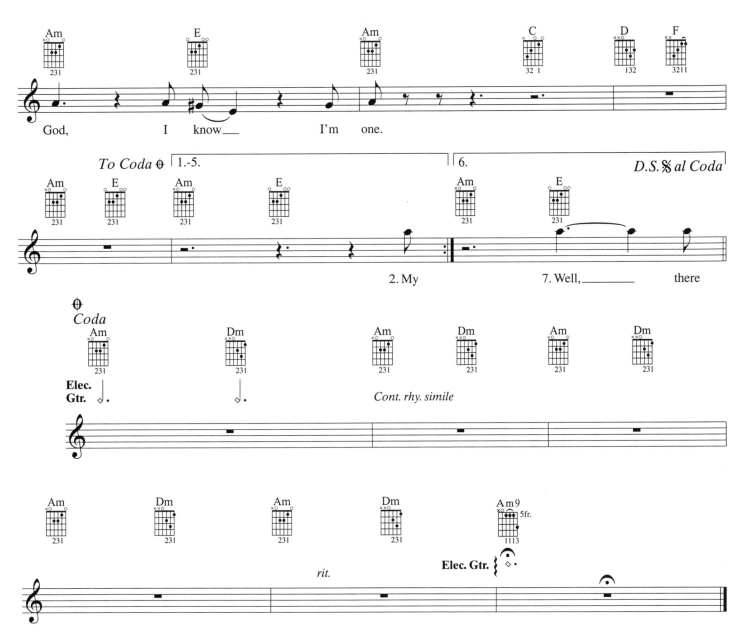

Verse 2:
My mother was a tailor,
She sewed my new blue jeans.
My father was a gambling man
Down in New Orleans.

Verse 3:
Now, the only thing a gambler needs
Is a suitcase and a trunk.
And the only time he's satisfied
Is when he's all drunk.
(To Organ Solo:)

Verse 5:
Oh mother, tell your children
Not to do what I have done.
Spend your life in sin and misery
In the house of the Rising Sun.

Verse 6:
Well, I got one foot on the platform,
The other foot on the train.
I'm going back to New Orleans
To wear that ball and chain.

The House of the Rising Sun - 2 - 2

LISTEN TO THE MUSIC

Words and Music by
TOM JOHNSTON

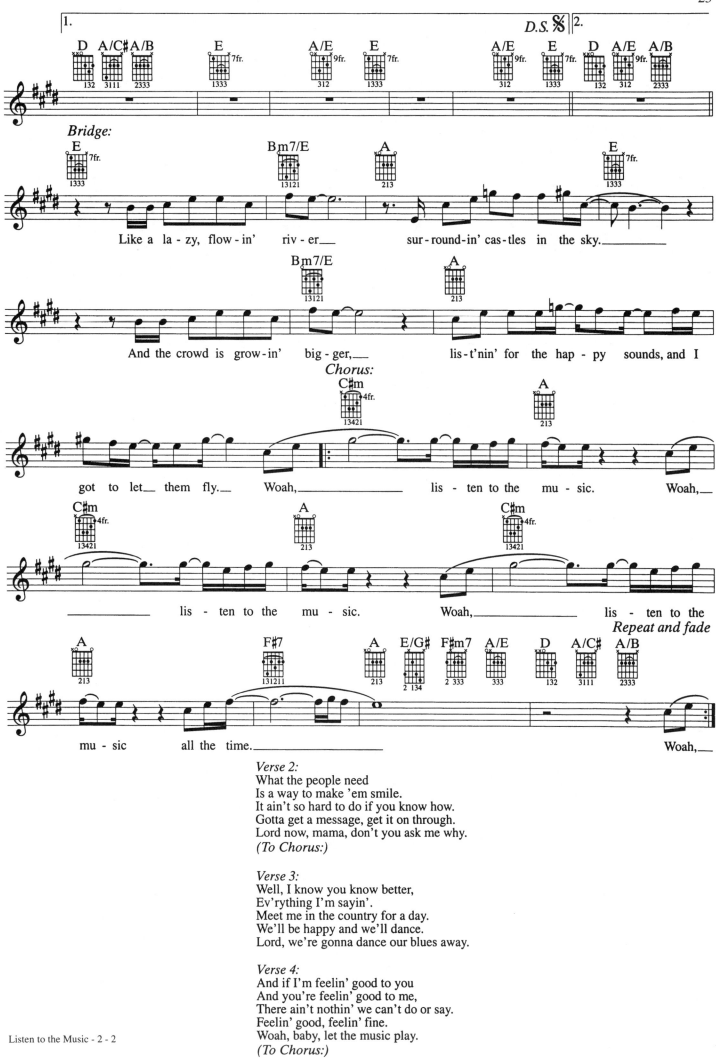

Verse 2:
What the people need
Is a way to make 'em smile.
It ain't so hard to do if you know how.
Gotta get a message, get it on through.
Lord now, mama, don't you ask me why.
(To Chorus:)

Verse 3:
Well, I know you know better,
Ev'rything I'm sayin'.
Meet me in the country for a day.
We'll be happy and we'll dance.
Lord, we're gonna dance our blues away.

Verse 4:
And if I'm feelin' good to you
And you're feelin' good to me,
There ain't nothin' we can't do or say.
Feelin' good, feelin' fine.
Woah, baby, let the music play.
(To Chorus:)

MAMA TOLD ME (NOT TO COME)

Words and Music by
RANDY NEWMAN

Moderately ♩ = 112
Intro:

Ab7

Elec. Piano *(arr. for gtr.)*

Band enters

1. *Want some*

Rhy. Fig. 1

Verse:
Elec. Piano cont. simile

Ab7

whis - key in your wa - ter, su - gar in your tea?
2. O - pen up the win - dow, let some air in - to this room.
3. Ra - di - o is blast - ing, some - one's knock - ing at the door.

What's all these cra - zy ques - tions they're ask - ing me?
I think I'm al - most chok - ing from the smell of stale per - fume.
I'm look - ing at my girl and she's passed out on the floor.

This is the cra - zi - est par - ty that could ev - er be.
And that cig - a - rette you're smok - in' don't scare me half to death.
I seen so man - y things I ain't nev - er seen be - fore.

Mama Told Me Not to Come - 4 - 1

Outro: w/ad lib. vocal
w/Rhy. Fig. 2 *(Elec. Gtr.) 1st 2 meas. only, 12 times, simile*

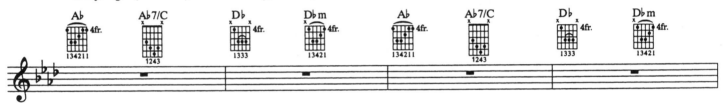

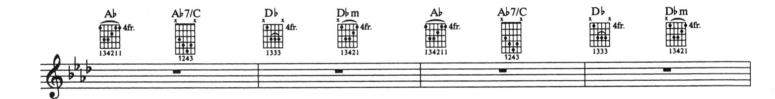

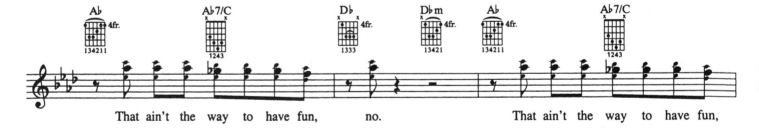

That ain't the way to have fun, no.   That ain't the way to have fun,

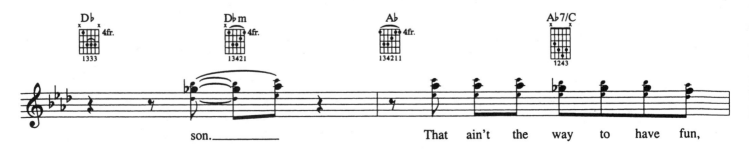

son._____   That ain't the way to have fun,

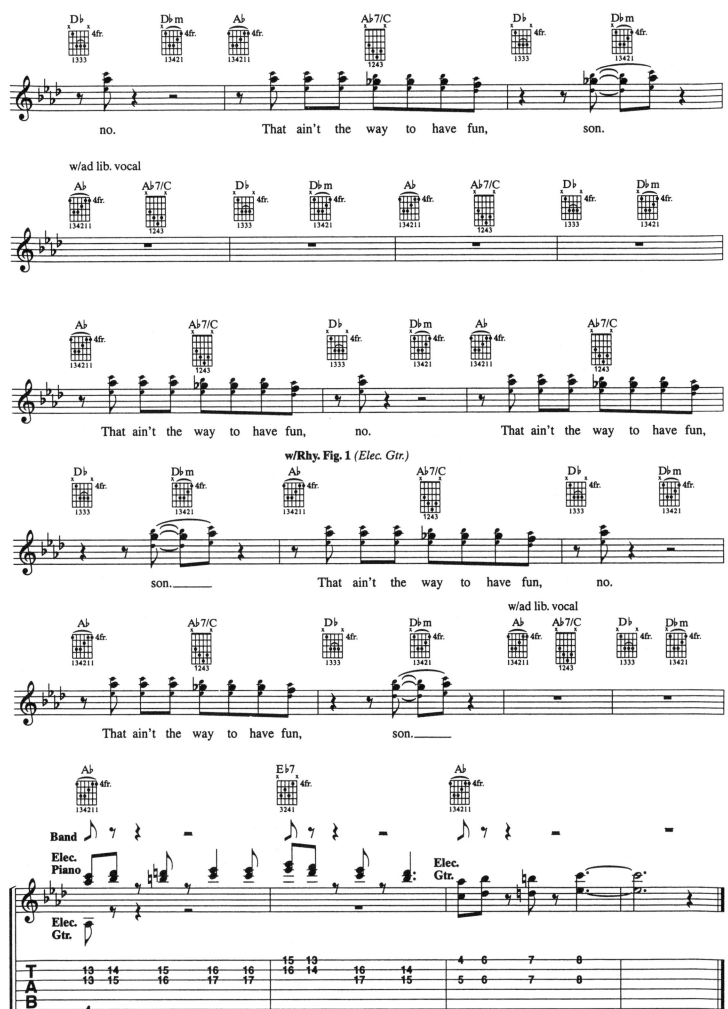

MY MUSIC

Words and Music by
JIM MESSINA and KENNY LOGGINS

29

Verse 2:
Hey, little girl, wanna dance with you all night long.
The music's got me buzzin' and I feel
Pretty loose, I feel the rhythm and it's comin' on strong.
Let me lay a little wisdom on you, baby, there's a power in the sound.
With everybody jumpin', we can bring the house down.
So let's get to gettin' while the gettin' is right
And roll with the rhythm tonight.
(To Chorus:)

My Music - 2 - 2

RAPID ROY (THE STOCK CAR BOY)

Words and Music by JIM CROCE

Rock and roll ♩ = 164

Intro:

(1.3.5.) Rap - id Roy,___ that stock___ car boy,___ he ___ too much to___ be - lieve.___

2.4. *See additional lyrics*

You know he al - ways got an ex - tra pack of cig - a - rettes rolled

up in his T - shirt sleeve.___ He got a tat - too on his arm that say "Ba -

- by", he got an - oth - er one that just say "Hey."___ But ev - 'ry

Verse 2:
Oh rapid Roy, that stock car boy,
He's the best driver in the land.
He say that he learned to race a stock car
By runnin' 'shine outta Alabam'.
Oh, the demolition derby
And the figure eight,
Is easy money in the bank
Compared to runnin' from the man
In Oklahoma City
With a five-hundred gallon tank.
(To Verse 3:)

Verse 4:
Yeah, Roy so cool, that racin' fool,
He don't know what fear's about.
He do a hundred thirty mile an hour
Smilin' at the camera
With a toothpick in his mouth.
He got a girl back home
Name of Dixie Dawn,
But he got honeys all along the way.
And you oughta hear 'em screamin'
For that dirt track demon in a '57 Chevrolet.
(To Verse 5:)

SHE'S NOT THERE

Words and Music by
ROD ARGENT

1. Well, no one told me a - bout___ her,_____ the way she lied.___
2. Well, no one told me a - bout___ her;_____ what could I do?___

Well, no one told me a - bout___ her,___ how man-y peo - ple cried.__ }
Well, no one told me a - bout___ her,___ though they all knew.__ }

But it's too

late to say you're sor - ry. How would I know,__ why should I care?__

Please don't both - er try'n' to find__ her, she's not there.__

She's Not There - 2 - 1

WATCHING THE RIVER RUN

Words and Music by
JIM MESSINA and KENNY LOGGINS

WOODSTOCK

Moderately ♩ = 112

Words and Music by
JONI MITCHELL

Woodstock - 3 - 1

Verse 2:
Well, then can I walk beside you? I have come to lose the smog.
And I feel as if a cog in something turning.
And maybe it's the time of year, yes, and maybe it's the time of man.
And I don't know who I am but life is for learning.
(To Chorus:)

Verse 3:
By the time we got to Woodstock, we were half a million strong,
And everywhere was a song and a celebration.
And I dreamed I saw the bomber jet planes riding shotgun in the sky,
Turning into butterflies above our nation.
(To Chorus:)

WILD NIGHT

Words and Music by
VAN MORRISON

42

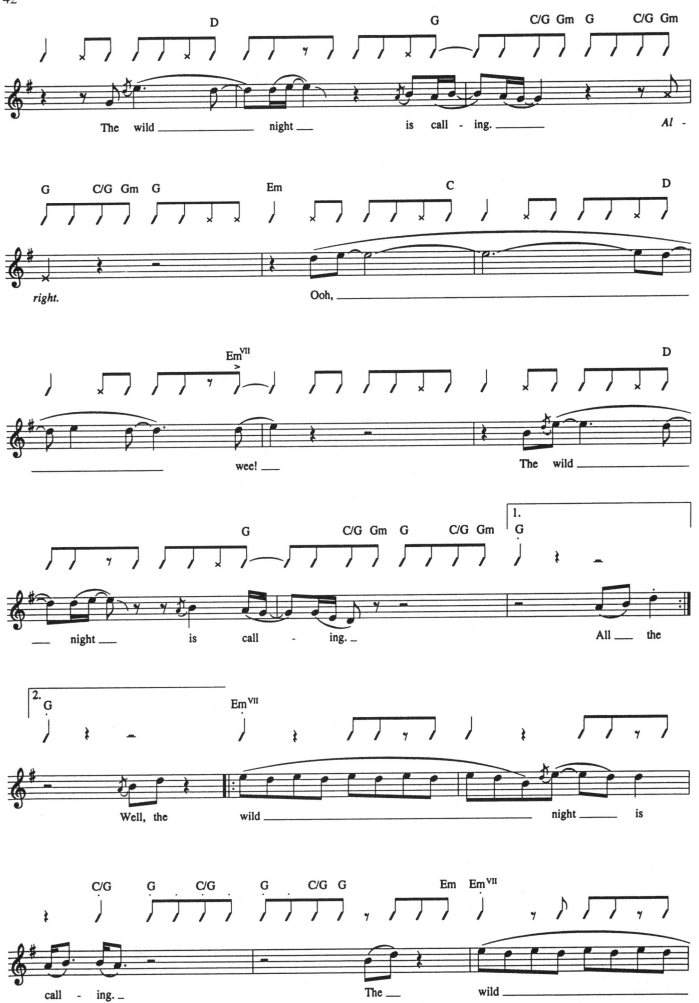

Verse 2:
And all the girls walk by, dressed up for each other.
And the boys do the boogie-woogie on the corner of the street.
And the people passin' by just stare in wild wonder.
And the inside juke-box roars out just like thunder.
−*(To Pre-chorus)*

Wild Night - 4 - 4

YOU REALLY GOT ME

Words and Music by
RAY DAVIES

* Original recording in A♭ major.

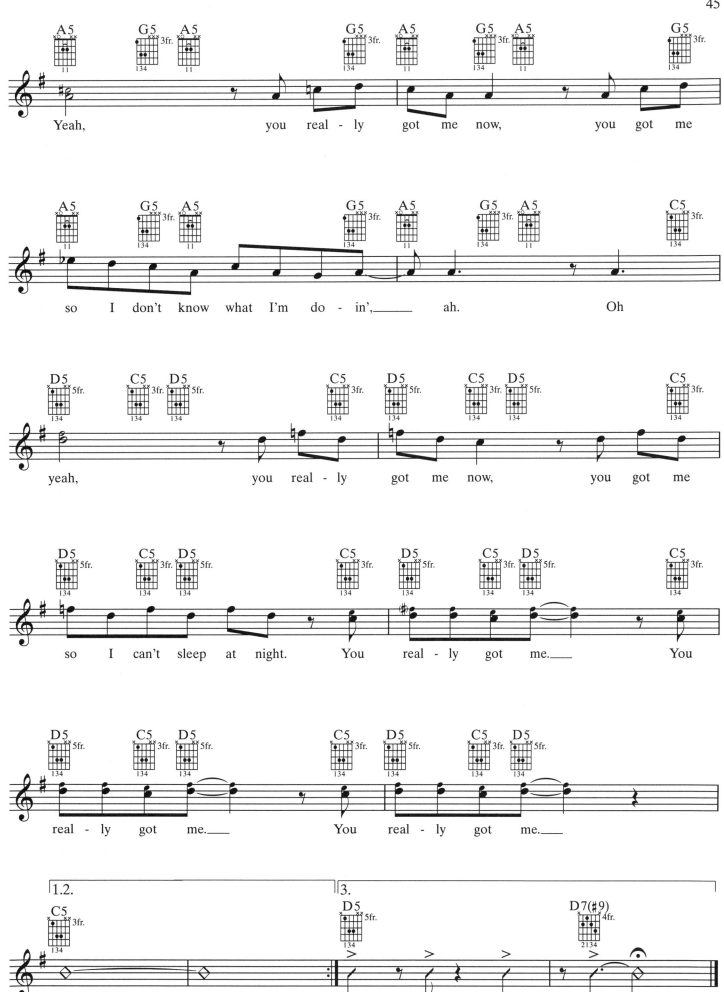

GUITAR TAB GLOSSARY **

TABLATURE EXPLANATION

READING TABLATURE: Tablature illustrates the six strings of the guitar. Notes and chords are indicated by the placement of fret numbers on a given string(s).

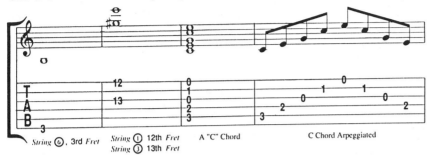

String ⑥, 3rd Fret   *String ① 12th Fret*   A "C" Chord   C Chord Arpeggiated
            String ③ 13th Fret

BENDING NOTES

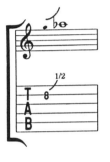

HALF STEP: Play the note and bend string one half step.*

WHOLE STEP: Play the note and bend string one whole step.

WHOLE STEP AND A HALF: Play the note and bend string a whole step and a half.

TWO STEPS: Play the note and bend string two whole steps.

SLIGHT BEND (Microtone): Play the note and bend string slightly to the equivalent of half a fret.

PREBEND (Ghost Bend): Bend to the specified note, before the string is picked.

PREBEND AND RELEASE: Bend the string, play it, then release to the original note.

REVERSE BEND: Play the already-bent string, then immediately drop it down to the fretted note.

BEND AND RELEASE: Play the note and gradually bend to the next pitch, then release to the original note. Only the first note is attacked.

BENDS INVOLVING MORE THAN ONE STRING: Play the note and bend string while playing an additional note (or notes) on another string(s). Upon release, relieve pressure from additional note(s), causing original note to sound alone.

BENDS INVOLVING STATIONARY NOTES: Play notes and bend lower pitch, then hold until release begins (indicated at the point where line becomes solid).

UNISON BEND: Play both notes and immediately bend the lower note to the same pitch as the higher note.

DOUBLE NOTE BEND: Play both notes and immediately bend both strings simultaneously.

*A half step is the smallest interval in Western music; it is equal to one fret. A whole step equals two frets.

**By Kenn Chipkin and Aaron Stang

RHYTHM SLASHES

STRUM INDICATIONS: Strum with indicated rhythm.

The chord voicings are found on the first page of the transcription underneath the song title.

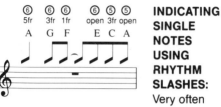

INDICATING SINGLE NOTES USING RHYTHM SLASHES: Very often single notes are incorporated into a rhythm part. The note name is indicated above the rhythm slash with a fret number and a string indication.

ARTICULATIONS

HAMMER ON: Play lower note, then "hammer on" to higher note with another finger. Only the first note is attacked.

LEFT HAND HAMMER: Hammer on the first note played on each string with the left hand.

PULL OFF: Play higher note, then "pull off" to lower note with another finger. Only the first note is attacked.

FRETBOARD TAPPING: "Tap" onto the note indicated by + with a finger of the pick hand, then pull off to the following note held by the fret hand.

TAP SLIDE: Same as fretboard tapping, but the tapped note is slid randomly up the fretboard, then pulled off to the following note.

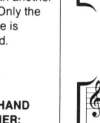

BEND AND TAP TECHNIQUE: Play note and bend to specified interval. While holding bend, tap onto note indicated.

LEGATO SLIDE: Play note and slide to the following note. (Only first note is attacked).

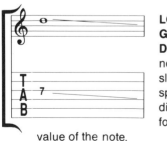

LONG GLISSANDO: Play note and slide in specified direction for the full value of the note.

SHORT GLISSANDO: Play note for its full value and slide in specified direction at the last possible moment.

PICK SLIDE: Slide the edge of the pick in specified direction across the length of the string(s).

MUTED STRINGS: A percussive sound is made by laying the fret hand across all six strings while pick hand strikes specified area (low, mid, high strings).

PALM MUTE: The note or notes are muted by the palm of the pick hand by lightly touching the string(s) near the bridge.

TREMOLO PICKING: The note or notes are picked as fast as possible.

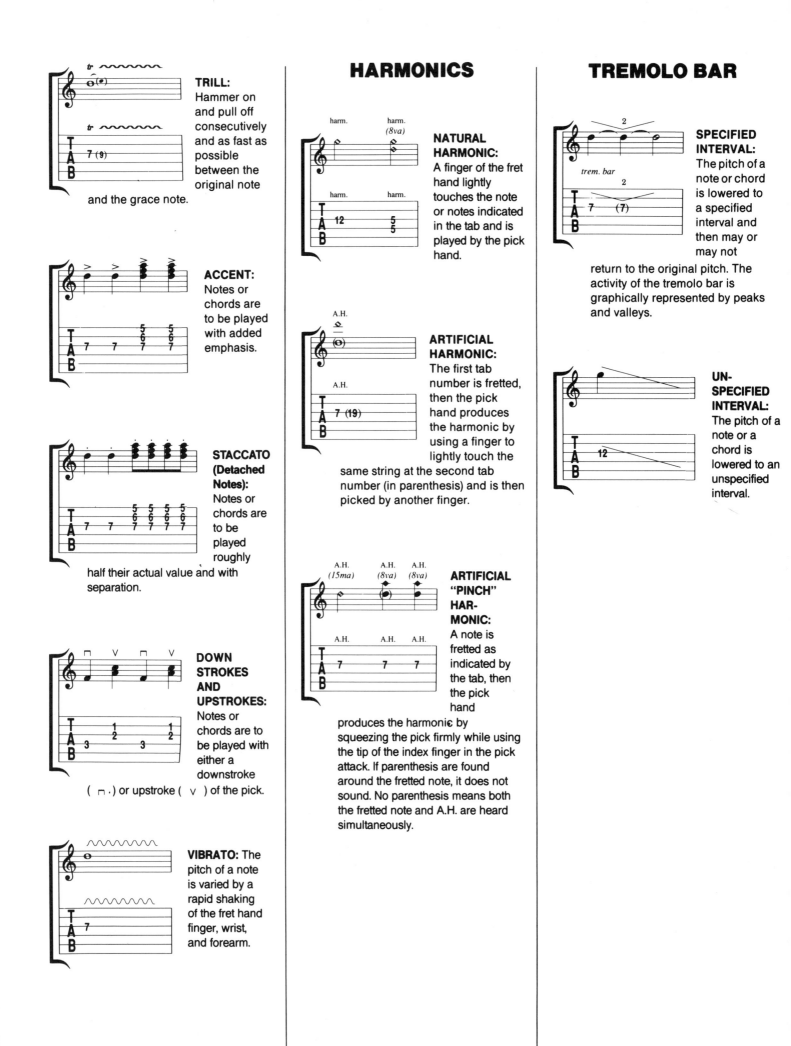

HARMONICS

TREMOLO BAR

TRILL: Hammer on and pull off consecutively and as fast as possible between the original note and the grace note.

ACCENT: Notes or chords are to be played with added emphasis.

STACCATO (Detached Notes): Notes or chords are to be played roughly half their actual value and with separation.

DOWN STROKES AND UPSTROKES: Notes or chords are to be played with either a downstroke (⊓ ·) or upstroke (∨) of the pick.

VIBRATO: The pitch of a note is varied by a rapid shaking of the fret hand finger, wrist, and forearm.

NATURAL HARMONIC: A finger of the fret hand lightly touches the note or notes indicated in the tab and is played by the pick hand.

ARTIFICIAL HARMONIC: The first tab number is fretted, then the pick hand produces the harmonic by using a finger to lightly touch the same string at the second tab number (in parenthesis) and is then picked by another finger.

ARTIFICIAL "PINCH" HAR-MONIC: A note is fretted as indicated by the tab, then the pick hand produces the harmonic by squeezing the pick firmly while using the tip of the index finger in the pick attack. If parenthesis are found around the fretted note, it does not sound. No parenthesis means both the fretted note and A.H. are heard simultaneously.

SPECIFIED INTERVAL: The pitch of a note or chord is lowered to a specified interval and then may or may not return to the original pitch. The activity of the tremolo bar is graphically represented by peaks and valleys.

UN-SPECIFIED INTERVAL: The pitch of a note or a chord is lowered to an unspecified interval.